YOUR KNOWLEDGE HAS VALUE

Bibliographic information published by the German National Library:

The German National Library lists this publication in the National Bibliography; detailed bibliographic data are available on the Internet at http://dnb.dnb.de .

Imprint:

Copyright © 2016 GRIN Verlag, Open Publishing GmbH
Print and binding: Books on Demand GmbH, Norderstedt Germany
ISBN: 9783656989400

This book at GRIN:

http://www.grin.com/en/e-book/335112/comparing-internally-consistent-human-resources-hrm-at-airport-express

Waseem Rauf

Comparing internally consistent Human Resources (HRM) at Airport Express Train (AET), Oslo, Norway and Southwest Airlines (SA), Dallas, TX, USA

GRIN Publishing

GRIN - Your knowledge has value

Since its foundation in 1998, GRIN has specialized in publishing academic texts by students, college teachers and other academics as e-book and printed book. The website www.grin.com is an ideal platform for presenting term papers, final papers, scientific essays, dissertations and specialist books.

Visit us on the internet:

http://www.grin.com/

http://www.facebook.com/grincom

http://www.twitter.com/grin_com

University of
Bedfordshire

University of Bedfordshire
MBA Mar' 16

Unit – Leading People in Organisations (SHR601-6)

Assessment 1 – Case Study

Comparing internally consistent Human Resources (HRM) at Airport Express Train (AET), Oslo, Norway and Southwest Airlines (SA), Dallas, TX, USA

Author:
Waseem Abdul Rauf

08th May 2016

Executive Summary

In today's competitive world of business, its very crucial and necessary to maintain the employees within the organisation and make sure that they are committed to work. This is very important because retaining employees within organisations has become frightening for many organisations.

This report has focused on 2 different companies namely Southwest Airlines (SA) and Airport Express Train (AET) where both the companies are operating in the travel sector. SA is an airline company based in USA whereas AET is an express train operating between Airport and Oslo, Norway. Both the companies were very different with regards to the size, age, ownership, competitive strategy, national context and labour laws. But eventually both the company achieved their competitive strategy and succeed through the application of High Performance Work System (HPWS).

The report was concluded where a critical analysis of the companies was carried out in relation to theories. SA and AET both were successful in their businesses throughout their past, but there needs to be some recommendation made in order for them to grow themselves and improve on flaws. Finally, recommendation on how to achieve the competitive advantage through employees were suggested to continue their success in the future.

Table of Contents

Introduction

This report will critically evaluate and examine the case study "Comparing internally consistent Human Resources (HRM) at Airport Express Train, Oslo, Norway and Southwest Airlines, Dallas, TX, USA" by Kuvaas and Dysvik (2012). It can be seen how both of these companies has been successful throughout their business and how they both have managed their employees using High Performance Work System (HPWS) and putting the theory into practice. The report will also identify and find out the main similarities and dissimilarities between SA and AET with respect to HR issues with respect to the age of the company, size of the company, ownership of the company, competitive strategy, national context and labour laws.

Moreover, the internal consistent of human resources management of these companies will be discussed and analysed throughout the report. HPWS is considered to be very fundamental and important for any organization in order to be successful in managing people effectively. According to Kuvaas and Dysvik (2012), it is proven that both the companies SA and AET have successfully applied the HPWS theory into their day to day activities at work.

According to Huselid (1995), progressive HR practices will result a company in getting higher organizational performance and it is also claimed that a set of HR practices is called as HPWS which in turn is related to better turnover, help in attaining more profits and finally an increased market value of the organization. However, Pfeffer (1998) argues that there are seven main characteristics of HPWS that are directly related with the internal consistent of HR in any organization. Following these characteristics is considered to make good profits and success to an organization.

Analysis

This chapter of the report will assess the comparison between the companies SA and AET where the internal consistent in HR will be explained and evaluated. This section also focuses on how both these companies were successful by applying HPWS theory into practice throughout their HR department.

Comparison of similarities and dissimilarities between SA and AET with respect to HR issues

Kuvaas and Dysvik (2012) explained in the case study that the main similarity between the both companies SA and AET is that they operate in the same travel industry. They have applied the HPWS theory into practice on HR functions within the organisation to be successful in the market.

Both the companies are different from each other with respect to the size, age, ownership, competitive strategy, national context and labour laws. It is proved that they have achieved their competitive advantage using HPWS into their HR practices (Kuvaas and Dysvik, 2012).

Moreover, both the companies were different from each other. SA was an airline based company in the USA whereas AET was an Airport railway service in the Norway. SA was a bigger company compared to AET with regards to the size of the organisation. The competitive strategy of SA was to provide better services to their customers with low cost whereas the competitive strategy of AET was to provide high quality service with high cost. But at the end of the day, both have achieved their competitive advantage by practicing HPWS (Kuvaas and Dysvik, 2012).

Another major difference between both the companies SA and AET as highlighted by Pfeffer (1998) is that SA provides job security to its employees where the SA management thinks that they don't want to put their best assets at risk and lose people in their organisation which is considered to be backbone of their company. Whereas, according to Lazear (1990), the national labour law of Norway itself provides the job security to all the employees working in the country.

Internal Consistency in HR between SA and AET

According to Pfeffer (1998), SA and AET both the companies have followed the HPWS in order for the organisation to achieve their competitive advantage.

SA has focused and maintained HPWS through their HR functions by giving more importance to the training provided to their employees, retaining those trained and skilled employees within the organisation and achieving success throughout their business. It is also proven that SA provides job security to their employees where the company do not risk themselves in losing the best assets of their company in the hands of competitors (Pfeffer, 1998).

AET maintains their HPWS in HR practices by focusing more and giving importance to selective hiring and then gradually training their employees to provide the utmost results. Whereas, AET did not provide the job security to their employees, which in turn according to Lazear (1990) were guaranteed by the Norway Labour Law (Pfeffer, 1998).

From the above, it can be understood that both the companies SA and AET had about the same internal consistent in achieving their respective competitive advantage. In both the companies, SA and AET had aligned their internal consistent vertically with the business strategy and horizontally aligned with the HR practices and functions (Pfeffer, 1998).

According to Barney (1991), the resource based view (RBV) model is used mainly to focus on strategic human resource development in order to achieve the competitive advantage of an organisation. The RBV critically evaluates the HR functions that are being performed in an organisation and helping the organisation in achieving better management strategically. The RBV model (figure 1) showcase the 4 major points, Value, Rarity, Inimitability and Non-substitutability where these are considered to be the resources of a company. Likewise, these resources will take shape until to the strategies where the company will have their competitive advantage and internal consistent. According to the figure, when the company has sustained their competitive advantage, the performance they can expect and have will be excellent.

SA also had the similar resources where they were able to achieve their competitive advantage (Barney, 1991).

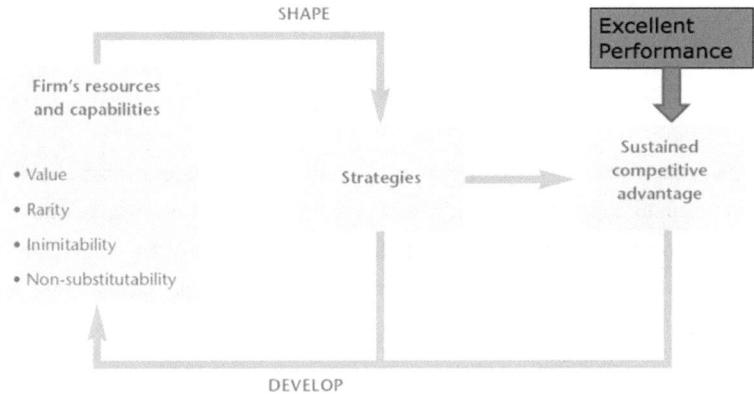

Figure 1: The relationship between resource endowments, strategies and sustained competitive advantage (Resource based View Model) (Barney, 1991)

Conclusion

This report has evaluated the similarities and dissimilarities between the companies SA and AET with respect to their HR issues. There was a comparison between the internal consistent in the HR of SA and AET with respect to the size, age, size, competitive strategy, labour law and national context. The report has highlighted their success story on how they are successful in the similar industry of travel using the HPWS and putting these HPWS into practice on their day to day HR functions.

SA gave importance to job security, selective hiring and training of their employees whereas AET focused on selective hiring and employee training. During the beginning of the report, it has been mentioned that both the companies SA and AET had different competitive strategy.

In conclusion, it can be said that through good HRM practices and HPWS any organisation regardless of their size or age or the industry they operate, they can become successful in managing the best assets of an organisation which is people and achieve the organisations competitive strategy. SA and AET is one kind of companies where there is less similarity between the companies, but have been successful through good HRM practices and HPWS.

Recommendation

In any organisation regardless of the industry they operate in, the most important and crucial step to take is to have a well maintained HRM strategies and well organised HR practices. The internal consistent in the HR should be constructed in such a way that the main aspects of company such as age, size, competitive strategy, ownership, national context and labour laws of that country is considered.

In order to achieve competitive advantage through the greatest asset of a company which is employees, Mathur (2015) has recommended the following figure 2.

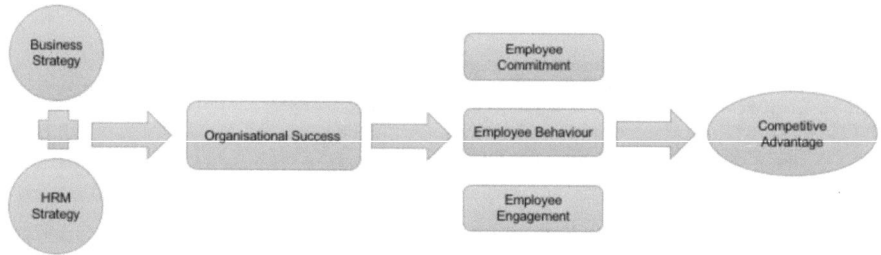

Figure 2: Achieving Competitive Advantage through Employees (Mathur, 2015)

According to Mathur (2015), a proper and successful alignment of Business Strategy and HRM Strategy will eventually lead to the success of an organisation. *"Employee plays a very important role in service delivery; employees can provide an edge of superior quality deliverance"* (Mathur, 2015). This explains that once the organisation is successful with the business strategy and HRM strategy, it's the employees who play an important and vital role in achieving more. The factors that support are Employee Commitment, Employee behaviour and Employee Engagement. Its not about the retention of employees at work, but its about encouraging and engaging those talented workforces at each and every stage at work. When all the above factors go hand in hand, it can be said that any organisation can achieve their competitive advantage (Mathur, 2015). SA and AET already gives importance to their employees and follow the best HRM strategies and practices to achieve their competitive advantage. But following the above recommendation can help them in growing more.

References

Barney, J. (1991). Firm resources and sustained competitive advantage. *Journal of Management, 17*(1), 99-120.

Huczynski, A. A. and Buchanan, D. A. (2013). Organizational Behaviour. 8th Ed. Pearson Education Limited, UK.

Huselid, M. A. (1995). The impact of human resource management practices on turnover, productivity, and corporate financial performance. *The Academy of Management Journal, 38*(3), 635-672.

Kuvaas, B. and Dysvik, A. (2012). 'Comparing Internally Consistent HR at the Airport Express Train, Oslo, Norway and Southwest Airlines, Dallas, TX, USA', A Case Study.

Lazear, E. P. (1990). Job security provisions and employment. *The Quarterly Journal of Economics,* August, 703-709.

Mathur, P. (2015). Achieving Competitive Advantage through Employees. *International Journal of Arts, Humanities and Management Studies, 01*(9), 66-71.

Pfeffer, J. (1998). The human equation: Building profits by putting people first. Harvard Business Press, USA.